CATHOLIC CHARISMATIC RENEWAL

by
Kristina Cooper

GW00658692

All boo
generous *support* *...*
Catholic Truth Society

CATHOLIC TRUTH SOCIETY
PUBLISHERS TO THE HOLY SEE

CONTENTS

INTRODUCTION

I regard it as a great privilege to have been asked to pen these few lines as an introduction to this booklet about the Catholic Charismatic Renewal. The author, Kristina Cooper, has been a close friend for many years, and through participation and observation she has built up a deep understanding and appreciation of this unusual working of the Holy Spirit in the lives of many millions of men and women around the world.

The Catholic Charismatic Renewal is often a controversial subject - people find it interesting and yet disturbing. They may have decided it's not for them, but are prepared to admit they don't really understand it. For some it's just one of the new movements in the Church, while others think it's all about prayer meetings. Many will immediately imagine people waving their arms in the air, babbling in tongues, behaving in what seems to be a very emotional way, and adopting a rather super-spiritual manner of speaking which seems to make very little sense to anyone else. Reports and photographs of charismatics in action may have convinced them that, whatever it may be about, they shouldn't have anything to do with it. They may have heard some story about a person who used to be quite normal, but has now gone completely over the top and become a religious fanatic. It is a great pity that the Charismatic Renewal so often produces these negative images and caricatures in people's minds - what about all the good things that have happened?

Most people know someone whose life has been changed for the better through their contact with the Charismatic Renewal. Many have come to a new, personal, living faith in Jesus Christ. Some have experienced physical or emotional healing, whilst others have returned to the Church and committed themselves to a renewed life of service. There has been a strong emphasis on prayer, the Scriptures, the Sacraments, and evangelisation, while new communities, missionary groups, and special services have been born. People notice these things, so they know there are good results. Why, then, do they still feel uneasy? Often the reasons are a combination of ignorance and fear, and this booklet will help to shed light on the ignorance and dispel the fear. For the truth is that the Charismatic Renewal is not just a special interest group which holds a weekly parish prayer meeting for people who like that sort of thing. At its heart lies the Baptism in the Holy Spirit - a grace of God freely offered to everyone. Through it we are invited to say a clear and definite yes to Jesus Christ, and to the empowering presence of the Holy Spirit in our lives. This will bring our faith alive in a new way, and equip us for greater service in the Church and in the world. But because we are creatures of habit and comfort, not many of us like the idea of challenge and change. This, combined with ignorance and a natural fear of the unknown and the unfamiliar, causes us to turn away from what is on offer - in spite the fact that the Church has clearly stated her acceptance and encouragement of the Catholic Charismatic Renewal.

So I am convinced that this little booklet is timely, and will help many people to a greater understanding and openness to this important action of God, so needed if we are to play our part in turning back the tide of secularisation which threatens to overwhelm us.

Charles Whitehead

(Charles Whitehead is the Chairman of the Catholic Charismatic Renewal Service Committee for England, and the past President of the International Services Council.)

WHAT IS CHARISMATIC RENEWAL?

It is estimated that over the last 35 years up to 120 million Catholics have been touched by the grace known as Charismatic Renewal. This has resulted in many active local Charismatic Renewal centres and groups all over the world, as well as new initiatives in evangelisation, prayer and Christian formation.

What holds all these different groups and people together is a shared spiritual experience known as "Baptism in the Spirit". The most distinguishing characteristic of Charismatic Renewal is perhaps its identification with the first Pentecost and belief that the role and the power of the Holy Spirit has not changed since then. Thus disciples of Christ today who open themselves to his Holy Spirit as the first apostles did, can experience the same power and receive the same gifts as they did, including gifts of healing, prophecy and tongues.

Unlike other, similar movements and communities which have flourished in the latter part of the last century, Charismatic Renewal as such doesn't really have a founder or a clear place or point in time when it all "began" or a formal membership or all encompassing structure.

Cardinal Suenens, one of the moderators of the Vatican II Council called it "a move of the Spirit" rather than a movement, as it affects people in different ways at all levels of faith. Talking of his own experience he once said, "I did not discover the Holy Spirit through the Renewal. The Spirit had long been at the centre of my faith. But the Renewal gave new life to my faith in the Spirit. I saw how some Christians live, who took the Acts of the Apostles at its word, and this led me to question the genuineness of my own faith. As a result I found that I believed in the action of the Holy Spirit but in a limited sphere."

This encounter released him into a greater experience and understanding of the work of the Holy Spirit and helped him to see the beginnings of the Church in a new light, giving him "a living example of that same faith for which I shall always be grateful." Many others have been similarly touched and Charismatic Renewal has helped to ignite, revitalise and renew the Christian faith of millions of people from all backgrounds round the world. Through this free action of the Holy Spirit they have been made aware of the love of God for them, the truth of the Gospel of Jesus Christ and the incredible transforming power of the Holy Spirit.

Biblical Roots

In the Acts of the Apostles *(Acts 1.8)* Luke recounts how Jesus promised his disciples that they would "receive power when the Holy Spirit comes upon you, and you will be my witnesses in Jerusalem throughout Judea and

Samaria, and to the ends of the earth." And after Pentecost this was what happened. The frightened apostles were transformed as the Holy Spirit fell upon them and they went out with new strength and power to preach the repentance of sins and the kingdom of God. Not only did they teach about Jesus but "awe came on everyone, and many wonders and signs were done through the apostles" too. Peter and John, for example healed the cripple at the temple gate "I have neither silver nor gold", said Peter to the man, "but what I do have I give you: in the name of Jesus Christ the Nazarene, rise up and walk." And he did. Philip does so many miracles in Samaria in Acts 8, that it arouses the jealousy of Simon the magician, who wants to have hands laid on him too so he can receive this power of the Holy Spirit and do similar things.

St Paul in his letters refers to these things too, as if the spiritual gifts and charisms were a normal part of the Christian experience. In the First Letter to the Corinthians Paul writes,"To each individual the manifestation of the Spirit is given for some benefit. To one is given through the Spirit the expression of wisdom, to another the expression of knowledge according to the same Spirit; to another gifts of healing by the one Spirit; to another mighty deeds; to another prophecy; to another discernment of spirits, to another varieties of tongues, to another interpretation of tongues." *(1 Corinthians 12:7-10)*

Even Paul's criticisms of the Corinthian church, that they were too concerned with the use of the spiritual gifts at the expense of love, shows that although the charisms could be pastorally problematic, they were considered part of Christian life. In chapter 14 of the First Letter to the Corinthians there is a long discourse about how the charism of prophecy is more useful than the gift of tongues and he writes, "I give thanks to God that I speak in tongues more than any of you, but in the church I would rather speak five words with my mind, so as to instruct others also, then ten thousand words in a tongue." *(1 Cor 14.18)*

Rediscovering the charisms
in the 20th century

Believing in things like charisms and the Holy Spirit's direct action in our lives doesn't come easily to Christians living in Western Europe. This is because our minds have often been more formed by the secularism of our culture than the biblical roots of our faith. This leads us to reject anything that cannot be explained by science. This rationalism, which we accept as the norm, however, is a comparatively recent phenomenon. You may be surprised to read St Bede's 'Ecclesiastical History of the English People' and at the way he writes in a very matter of fact way about the role prophecy, dreams and miracles played in the social and political history of England. This is something one cannot imagine historians writing today, as any action of God would be seen as opinion not fact.

Throughout the history of the Church however, extraordinary charisms have regularly appeared in the lives of saints right up until the present day, with people like Padre Pio for example who was famous for his healing miracles and words of knowledge. It is noticeable however, that following the Enlightenment in the 18th century, the rationalism it encouraged affected the spirituality of the Church too. The supernatural in all its forms was felt to be primitive and outdated and spiritual phenomena were discouraged and even suppressed. This was coupled with an over exaggerated stress on the Sacraments and the works dimension of Christian faith following the Reformation. Theologically too, the Holy Spirit tended to be the forgotten member of the Trinity and there was little written or preached about his role in helping people to live the Christian life. It was this growing institutionalisation of the Church that prompted Pope John XXIII in 1959 to call the Second Vatican Council and to pray that the Holy Spirit would renew his wonders "in this our day as by a new Pentecost." Charismatic Renewal can be seen as a response to this heartfelt prayer and a sovereign work of God to bring alive people's faith and restore the biblical charisms to normal Church life.

Ecumenical Roots

It was meditating on the Scriptures that led a group of Methodists, at a small bible college in Topeka, Kansas at the turn of the 20th century to wonder what had happened to the biblical charisms. Noticing that in the Acts of the Apostles every time the Spirit was asked for, people had hands laid on them, the group decided to do the same and they prayed for an outpouring of the Spirit as at the first Pentecost. To their astonishment they began to speak in tongues and prophesy like the first apostles.

Although their experience was not accepted by their denominational leaders, their minister Charles Parnham was certain they had discovered something valuable and continued to preach about it and encouraged people to be open to this Pentecostal experience. News of what had happened spread and in 1906 there was a spontaneous revival in a mixed ethnic Church in Los Angeles. This led eventually to the formation of a new Christian denomination where this experience, known as 'Baptism in the Spirit' and the biblical charisms were promoted and encouraged. Because of the link to Pentecost and the associated phenomena they became known as the Pentecostals.

In the 1950s David Du Plessis, a Pentecostal leader from South Africa felt led by God to share about these pentecostal graces with leaders from the World Council of Churches. Through personal contacts like these under-

standing and experience of the charisms gradually began
to seep into the mainline Protestant Churches. These
Christians felt what they had experienced was the fullness
of the Christian experience and not something that con-
tradicted their own religious tradition. Thus instead of
joining the Pentecostals, they stayed within their own
denominations and called themselves charismatic to sig-
nal this new experience and insight.

The new spirit of openness brought about by Vatican
II in the 1960s eventually led Catholics to meet and pray
with these Pentecostals and Charismatics of various traditions and it was through these encounters that Catholics
first began to hear about "the Baptism in the Spirit" and
the charisms that are available to all Christians who are
open to them.

The beginnings of the Charismatic Renewal in the Catholic Church - The Duquesne weekend

Although various Catholics had experienced "Baptism in
the Spirit" through their own ecumenical contacts, it was
the Duquesne weekend that really launched the
Charismatic Renewal in the Catholic Church. This was a
retreat organised for 24 students from the Chi Rho society
of Duquesne university in Pittsburgh. Two of their lecturers had already been touched by this pentecostal grace
and had invited a Charismatic Episcopalian woman to
share her experiences with the students. The students

were not told beforehand what to expect but to prepare themselves by reading "The Cross and the Switchblade" the true story of a Pentecostal minister and the amazing way the Holy Spirit had helped him in his work among the gangs of New York. They were also told to meditate on the first four chapters of the book of Acts.

Patti Gallagher Mansfield, one of the students wrote, "I naturally thought the weekend would be profitable but I must admit I never thought it would change my life. I found it intriguing, but a little hard to believe, when I was told that the charismatic gifts given to the apostles are still given today - that there are still signs and wonders - and that God has promised to pour forth his spirit on all flesh".

On the Saturday night a party had been arranged and Patti went to the chapel to encourage people to come into it. She remembers, "Then something happened that I wasn't expecting. I had always believed by the gift of faith that Jesus is really present in the Blessed Sacrament, but I had never experienced his glory before. As I knelt there that night my body literally trembled before his majesty and holiness. I was filled with awe in His presence. He was there... I felt really frightened and I said to myself, "Get out of here quick, because something is going to happen to you if you stay in the presence of God. And yet overriding this fear was the desire to remain before the Lord."

She prayed a deep prayer of unconditional surrender to God and found herself on the floor, prostrate before the Blessed Sacrament." I don't know exactly how it took place, but in the process, my shoes came off my feet. Later I realised that, like Moses before the burning bush I was indeed upon holy ground. As I lay there, I was flooded from my fingertips to my toes with a deep sense of God's personal love for me." Patti remembers two friends asking her afterwards, "'What happened to you? Your face looks different'. I didn't realise that I looked different, but apparently these girls saw a reflection in my face of what God had done in my heart."

That night over half the students - about a dozen people - had some kind of deep experience of the Holy Spirit. In her book 'As By a New Pentecost' Patti tells the story of the weekend, the events that led up to it and the different experiences the students had. Some students even missed out because they had gone to bed or didn't go to the chapel. Afterwards those students who had been touched by the Holy Spirit that night formed a charismatic prayer meeting where they began to practise the use of the gifts, first quite stumblingly. Patti recounts how she was nervously led by the Holy Spirit to go and pray for her housemother who was ill in hospital.

Ralph Martin and Steve Clark two leaders from Cursillo, a lay movement in the Catholic Church, heard what happened at Duquesne and came with others to find out for themselves. Ralph, recognised in this charismatic experience something of a similar private spiritual experience he had had and they all had hands laid on them for the release of the Holy Spirit in their lives. That summer a group of Duquesne students, including Patti, joined Ralph and Steve in campus evangelism, sharing what had happened and encouraging people to open their lives up to the Holy Spirit. The Charismatic Renewal was by now taking hold in the Catholic Church and charismatic prayer groups began to spring up and multiply.

Life in the spirit

Ralph and Steve, with their background in Cursillo and Christian discipleship, however, realised that some kind of vehicle was needed to channel and encourage this Pentecostal grace. Between them and with the help of others they produced "The Life in the Spirit Seminars". This was a simple seven session course that re-proclaimed the basic gospel message, the importance of conversion, and opened people up to the expectation of a visible working of the Holy Spirit in their lives through being "Baptised in the Spirit". Those touched by the Holy Spirit in this way began to meet in prayer meetings, where the emphasis was on singing, the sharing of faith stories, openness to the charisms and bible sharing and exposition. Thus the Charismatic Renewal began to spread rapidly round the world, as people shared with each other their experiences and asked to be prayed with so that the Holy Spirit could be released more in their lives.

One of the hallmarks of Charismatic Renewal ever since has been a mixture of organised outreach in the form of Life in the Spirit Seminars, when people have hands laid on them for the release of the Holy Spirit in their lives, and spontaneous personal private experiences where people only understand what has happened to them when they meet with others who have had a similar experience.

It was this need to meet with others and pray and share their experiences that led to the setting up of the first prayer groups. To provide more teaching larger gatherings were also organised on an ad hoc basis in some areas. These became known as Days of Renewal. Then, to get some kind of network and order, various committees on diocesan, national and international level were set up to facilitate communication and teaching between all these mushrooming groups. Once again this was very spontaneous rather than something centrally directed because no one was formally 'in charge.'

English Roots of the Catholic Charismatic Renewal

In England although some people had heard about the American experience, others came across Charismatic Renewal themselves through their own local ecumenical contacts. Simon Tugwell OP, for example a Dominican, from Oxford, had begun praying with Pentecostals and discovered the charisms through them and began an ecumenical prayer meeting which was very influential in the early days of Charismatic Renewal in the South of England. Others joined him and more and more Roman Catholics were brought into this Pentecostal experience of the charisms. Bob Balkam, an American with experience of the Catholic Charismatic Renewal in the United States, who had contacts in England, was persuaded to come to Britain and provide some wisdom and leadership. He later became the chairman of the first National Service Committee for Catholic Charismatic Renewal that was set up in 1974.

This lack of a clearly identifiable human founder with a clear moral authority has continued to mark the development of the Charismatic Renewal. It also helps to explain why Catholic Charismatic Renewal has developed into so many different forms and spiritual expressions according to the historic circumstances in which it finds itself and the people involved. Like the Church itself those in Charismatic Renewal span both left and right wing politically, and can be theologically either liberal or conservative. There are those who are also very marian or traditional in their spirituality and others who are more influenced by an evangelical worldview. For each their personal situation and circumstances has had an effect on how the initial grace has been lived out and expressed.

BAPTISM IN THE SPIRIT AND ITS EFFECTS

Baptism in the Holy Spirit

The central grace of the Charismatic Renewal is what is known as "Baptism in the Spirit". As this is an expression that has been inherited from the Pentecostal tradition, it can be confusing for Catholics as it seems to imply that you haven't been validly baptised and need a second baptism. This is not true of course but "Baptism in the Spirit" remains difficult to categorise precisely and theologically. Those who have experienced it, however, know the difference it has made to their lives. They begin to experience the sense of God being their father, they come into a personal relationship with Jesus Christ and experience the Holy Spirit guiding and directing them in their lives. This new openness to the Holy Spirit often leads to the discovery of the biblical charisms as outlined in St Paul's Letters to the Corinthians *(1 Cor.12.4-11)*; Romans *(12.6-8)* and Ephesians *(4.8 and 11)*. Instead of these being interesting historical phenomena, they become something of use today.

I know the difference "baptism in the spirit" made in my own life. Although I had always been a practising Catholic I had no inner spiritual life. I never read the bible, I rarely prayed and for me God was very remote, more of a concept than a person with no involvement in our world. Although I was technically a Catholic, in practice my lifestyle was that of a secular humanist. When I was in my late twenties searching for something more I went to Panama in Central America. There I came across a charismatic prayer group, who challenged me with their vivid belief in a God who was intimately interested and involved in their everyday life. They encouraged me to read the Acts of the Apostles. This led to me praying in a chapel on the feast of Pentecost for God to reveal himself to me and baptise me in his Holy Spirit like the first apostles. That night I had a profound experience of God. I became aware for the first time of my sinfulness and pride and the way in which, although I had lived outwardly a very moral life, I had lived for myself and not for Christ. I repented and vowed to God henceforth to live my life for Him. The fruit of this new relationship with Jesus Christ was an overwhelming desire to pray, to read the bible, and to get to know God more. It was as if the veil was lifted from my eyes and I began to see God's action everywhere and I wanted to tell everyone about Him. I realised from personal experience that Christ was the answer to all the great hungers of the human heart and I wanted to serve Him.

Others who have been touched by the Charismatic Renewal have similar stories and experiences to tell. Some are incredibly dramatic - of drug addicts healed and reformed through the power of God, or physical and

emotional healings or simply a new sense of mission
and vocation in a person's life. Fr Raniero Cantalamessa
OFM Cap, who has been the preacher to the Pope and
the papal household for the last 20 years, was 43 years
old and a leading Franciscan academic when he was
baptised in the Spirit in the 1970s. He considers this
experience the watershed of his spiritual life and even
now sees everything in terms of before and after this
event. Afterwards he felt impelled to go out and tell
people about Jesus Christ and, with the permission of
his order, he left his job as a professor at Milan university so that he could go on the road, giving retreats and
preaching the gospel.

He was initially very sceptical about Charismatic
Renewal. But when he attended a charismatic prayer
meeting for the first time he was very touched by what he
saw. He remembers, "Studying the history of ancient
Christianity as I did, I could understand what was happening in these meetings. For they were in fact very similar to
what happened in the first Christian communities in the
early Church. Yet I could see that it was something spontaneous and not done in imitation of them. I could see that
it was a real thing, although going on in a new fashion."

What is Baptism in the Spirit?

Fr Cantalamessa believes that while it is not a sacrament, Baptism in the Spirit is related to the sacraments

of initiation. He comments that for many people these sacraments though valid, remain "tied." This means that the graces from them are impeded, due to lack of response on the part of the person concerned. Sacraments, he insists are not magical rituals which act automatically but they do require a response. Thus in our secular society with the practice of infant baptism and confirmation, people can grow up being sacramentalised but not evangelised. Fr Cantalamessa believes that Baptism in the Spirit is a grace sent by God in our time to "untie" these sacraments of baptism and confirmation and reactivate in the individual the witness to faith that the sacraments are supposed to produce.

What the Fathers of the Church Say

Fr Killian McDonnell OSB, a theologian, is convinced that "Baptism in the Spirit" and its accompanying charisms should be the normal experience for all Christians. He has found writings in the patristic fathers to support this view. Hilary of Poitiers for example writes, "We who have been reborn through the sacrament of baptism experience intense joy when we feel within us the first stirring of the Holy Spirit. We begin to have insight into the mysteries of faith, we are able to prophesy and to speak with wisdom. We become steadfast in hope and receive the gift of healing."

Fr Raniero Cantalamessa OFM, Preacher to the Papal Household.

Cyril of Jerusalem in his baptismal lectures to the cate-
chumens in the Church of Jerusalem mentions the importance of preparing to receive the charism of prophecy. He
concludes, "My final words beloved ones, in this instruc-
tion are words of exhortation, urging you to prepare your
souls for the reception of the heavenly charisms." For
many of these writers, the charisms, including the extraordinary ones, were seen as something to be expected following the rite of Christian initiation.

Fr Peter Hocken, a historian of the charismatic renewal, however, believes that the Baptism in the Spirit has a
deeper significance than just making Catholics more alive
in their faith and open to the charismatic gifts. He
believes that its ecumenical roots this century are an
intrinsic part of its role and calling. He feels it is significant that the same spiritual experience and phenomena
have happened in all the Christian traditions creating a
special sense of unity among them. He stresses, "If we
lose the ecumenical dimension we also risk losing the
fullness of what God is doing. It is not just a matter of
God restoring the charisms to the Roman Catholic
Church, but what he is doing in the whole body of Christ.
By people trying to insist on Catholic explanations for
what is happening, the danger is that we do not do justice
to the full spiritual reality of the charismatic renewal and
thus weaken it as a spiritual force and blunt its prophetic
edge." He believes that the Charismatic Renewal and the

way it has effected people in all the different denominations in the same way, has a particular eschatalogical significance. This is ultimately to restore unity to the body of Christ to prepare for the second coming of Christ.

THE CHARISMATIC GIFTS

It would seem that one of the purposes of the Holy Spirit in raising up the Charismatic Renewal in the Church is to restore the use of the charismatic gifts to the normal life of the Church, just as they were in use at the beginning of its history. As can be seen in the Book of Acts and St Paul's letters, this empowering with the gifts of the Holy Spirit made the early Christians very effective, as they went about healing the sick, prophesying and being prompted by the Holy Spirit in their decisions. This is something we need very much today if we are to carry out the New Evangelisation called for by the Pope.

Lists of the gifts of the Holy Spirit or charisms as they are also known, can be found in 1 Corinthians 12:7-12; Romans 12:6-9 and Ephesians 4:7-14. Corinthians mentions nine spiritual gifts. These include the gifts of wisdom, knowledge, faith, healing, miracles, prophecy, discernment of spirits, tongues and interpretation of tongues. These charisms are not a sign of personal holiness or spiritual maturity. Rather they are to help equip Christians for service in the Church and the world. Unlike natural gifts they are not under the control of the person using them. Thus there is always an element of risk as someone has to step out in faith when they believe God is calling them to exercise a particular gift. The gifts also always have to be discerned for it is ultimately by their spiritual and practical fruits that you can tell if they are genuine or not. As someone once said, "It's easy to know if God has given you the charism of healing - people get healed when you pray for them."

Tongues

Perhaps the most controversial of the spiritual gifts is the gift of tongues which to the average person can look like emotional meaningless babble. It does have a firm basis in the New Testament, however and in Mark 16:17 we read that Jesus said that believers "will speak in new tongues". This happened on the day of Pentecost and in Acts 10:44 at the house of Cornelius. "While Peter was still speaking, the Holy Spirit fell upon all who heard the word. The circumcised believers who had come with Peter were astounded that the gift of the Holy Spirit had been poured out on the Gentiles, for they heard them speaking in tongues and extolling God." It also happened at Ephesus; "When Paul had laid his hands on them, the Holy Spirit came upon them, and they spoke in tongues and prophesised." *(Acts 19:6).*

There are various types of manifestations of tongues. Sometimes as at Pentecost someone can speak a language they have never learnt, but this is very uncommon and is usually a few words of consolation for someone who needs to hear them in their own language. Sometimes at a prayer meeting a prophecy can be given in tongues, which is then is followed by an interpretation in English. The most common form at charismatic gatherings, however, is communal singing in tongues which can be very beautiful and seems to spontaneously start and finish. But as St Paul suggests in 1 Corinthians 14 tongues is primarily for private prayer.

The main benefit of tongues is that it opens people up to the non-rational and is a gift of surrender to the Holy Spirit. As it says in Romans 8:26 "In the same way the Spirit too comes to the aid of our weakness; for we do not know how to pray as we ought, but the Spirit itself intercedes with inexpressible groanings. And the one who searches hearts knows what is the intention of the Spirit, because it intercedes for the holy ones according to God's will." And it is at times like these when words don't seem enough that tongues is such a great help. This is why Fr Robert Faricy SJ, professor of Spirituality at the Gregorian University in Rome likes to refer to it as "noisy contemplation."

The more rational and in control a person is, the more difficult it can be for them to be released into the gift of tongues, because they keep on wanting to understand what is happening, and this becomes a block to them actually receiving it. I believe I received the gift of tongues when I was baptised in the Holy Spirit, many years ago, but as I didn't know what was happening, I did not co-operate with it. I remember I felt I wanted to say something to God but had no words or thoughts to ver-balise so although I felt my tongue wanting to move, I said nothing. It was only later when I started mixing and talking to other people involved in Charismatic Renewal that I realised what it was, although it took another five months for me to be open enough to yield to it again.

Dr Dan Montgomery, a clinical psychologist com-ments, "I believe that speaking in tongues involves a hemispherical shift from left brain thinking and speech production to right brain surrender and creativity. This is similar to the shift from left brain to right brain we expe-rience when we hold a new born infant. We don't say, "This is a fine looking specimen of humanity." We utter oohs and ahs." He also believes that praying in tongues brings relaxation and serenity, and had direct experience of this while at graduate school when he was hooked up to a sophisticated machine for measure brain wave pat-terns and muscle tension while praying in tongues

Once you discover you have the gift of tongues it is not something that takes you over, as some people fear, but you can decide when you want to use it the way you would any other language. I have found that the gift of tongues is a gateway to communication with the Holy Spirit and it can be useful of many occasions when you don't know what to pray for but need God's help. This happens a lot when you are praying for healing and doesn't know how to pray for the person. It can also be useful in other situations. I remember once I was alone in a railway compartment with a group of drunken football supporters and felt very vulnerable. I prayed in tongues. A few minutes later as I was reading the Mass reading for the following day, I received what I felt was an inner prompting that I should share this passage of scripture with these men. Worried that it was just my imagination, I promised God I would only do it if the men came down and sit next to me - which three of them did a short while later. Helped by the Holy Spirit I was able to speak to them and to my amazement they were very open and we had a very meaningful conversation about God.

Tongues not only appears in the Scriptures but also in the history of Church, particularly in the writings of St Augustine and St Teresa of Avila in her book the *Sixth Dwelling Place* (Chapter 6:10-12) counsels her sisters about it. "Our Lord sometimes gives the soul feelings of jubilation and a strange prayer it doesn't understand. I am writing about this favour here so that if He grants it to you, you may give Him such praise and know what is taking place. It is, in my opinion, a deep union of the faculties, but our Lord nonetheless leaves them free that they might enjoy this joy - and the same goes for the senses - without understanding what it is they are enjoying or how they are enjoying."

"It seems like gibberish and certainly the experience is like that, for it is a joy so excessive that the soul wouldn't want to enjoy it alone but wants to tell everyone about it so that they might help this soul praise our Lord.. I knew a saint named Friar Peter of Alacantara - for I believe from the way he lived that he was one - who did this very thing, and those who at one time listened to him thought he was crazy. Oh what blessed sadness, sisters! If only God would give it to us all! And what a favour He has granted you by bringing you to his house where, when the Lord gives you this favour and you tell others about it, you will receive help rather than the criticism you would receive in the world."

Prophecy

St Paul counsels the early Church to "Pursue love and strive for the spiritual gifts, and especially that you may prophesy."*(1 Corinthians 14:1)* and later "Those who prophesy speak to other people for their upbuilding and encouragement and consolation."

There are various other examples of prophecy in action in the book of Acts. For example when Agabus predicts that there will be a severe famine *(Acts 11:27-30)*, which helps galvanise the early Church to raise funds to support their fellow believers in Judea. Likewise in Antioch it mentions that there are teachers and prophets and it mentions in Acts 13:1-3 how "when they were worshipping the Lord and fasting, the Holy Spirit said, "set apart for me Barnabas and Saul for the work to which I have called them. Then completing their fasting and prayer, they laid hands on them and sent them off."

The gift of prophecy has various aspects. Its main role is to proclaim the word of God in a particular situation or to a person and one can think of prophetic Catholic figures in our society today, like the Catholic peer Lord Alton, who call society to come back to godly values. In a prayer group the prophetic word is usually more personal and usually happens when someone shares a piece of scripture in the group and finds that it is particularly appropriate to someone there. Often it might simply be a word of consolation but because of its timing, the person concerned experiences it as a direct communication from God himself. This helps to increase the person's sense of a God who intimately cares for them and is with them in their situation.

Sometimes whole groups can receive a word of scripture that is particularly relevant to them and which they feel they must act on. A famous example of this was in the 1970s in El Paso in New Mexico, when a nun with a prophetic ministry quoted from Matthew's gospel Jesus's teaching about inviting to your table the poor and those who can not repay you. The group under the leadership of Fr Rick Thomas, a Jesuit, felt this was a specific word of God to them, which they had to obey. Thus on Christmas Eve they went to share a Christmas meal with the rag pickers living on the rubbish dump in Guarrez across the border in Mexico. An extraordinary miracle happened. That night they experienced a modern feeding of the 5000, when the food they had brought multiplied before their eyes and they found they were able to feed all those who came, despite the fact there were double the numbers they had catered for. This phenomenon of multiplication of food, together with healings, has been a constant in the work and life of the ministry that evolved at the dump since then. The full story can be found in the book '*The Miracles of El Paso*' by Fr Rene Laurentin and on the video '*Viva Cristo Rey*' produced by the community God's Delight in Texas. The details of ongoing mini-miracles appear in the newsletter of Fr Rick Thomas's community's ministry to the dump. For example there was a story of a man who came with a box of oranges to give to the poor at the dump. To his chagrin, he realised there wouldn't be enough but prayed they would stretch as far as possible. He intended to give only one orange per person, but felt an inner prompting to give two. He obeyed this not daring to look in the box. But he found when he reached the end of the line, that not only had everyone received two oranges but the box was still two thirds full!

Making the impossible Possible

On rare occasions prophetic words are given which are about the future. An example of this happened in

Nicaragua in 1998, where the City of God, a Christian community, was warned beforehand about a coming hurricane (Hurricane Mitch). This enabled them to take precautions and meant they were equipped to help others when the hurricane happened.

Prophetic words can also be helpful in giving people the courage to step out and do something that seems impossible using common sense. New Dawn, a charismatic conference that takes place in Walsingham every summer, for example, was started through a prophetic word received by Myles Dempsey, the leader of a small Catholic lay community. Impressed by a large charismatic gathering in Ars in France, he asked God if he wanted something similar in England, and received back the words "New Dawn" and "Walsingham". Although he and his community had no resources or experience, helped by the Holy Spirit, they were able to organise a gathering that today attracts over 2000 people. The Celebrate conference, which takes place at a holiday camp at Easter every year, also began with a word of prophecy. This helped the organisers, a group of committed lay Catholics led by a Charles Whitehead, a leader in Charismatic Renewal, to step out in faith and risk putting down a substantial deposit when they were not sure beforehand if anyone would come and if they would meet their costs. Once again their faith was richly rewarded and the conference was and continues to be a great success, attracting up to 1200 people for teaching and fellowship.

Prophecy has to be discerned, however, as there is always a human element within it which needs to be recognised and allowed for. This is why the word of the prophet is not enough and the prophecy always has to be discerned by those in authority who have pastoral responsibility for the community. In a Catholic context these will often be bishops or priests. True prophecy moreover will never contradict scripture or church teaching. Also if it is about some practical action, it will usually confirm or give guidance in an area that is already under consideration in some way, rather than being something coming right out of the blue. As Paul says, "Do not quench the Spirit. Do not despise the words of the prophets, but test everything; hold fast to what is good." *(1 Thessalonians 5:19)*

Healing

Jesus not only healed the sick himself but he commanded his disciples to do the same in his name. "And he called the twelve together and gave them power and authority over all demons and to cure diseases, and he sent them out to preach the kingdom of God and to heal. And they departed and went through the villages, preaching the gospel and healing everywhere."*(Luke 9:1)* (cf. *Luke 10:9* for the seventy). Jesus also promised that "these signs will accompany those who believe: in my name they will cast out demons... they will lay their hands on the sick, and they will recover." *(Mark 16:17)*. And St Paul lists the "gift of healing" as one of the gifts of the Holy Spirit. *(1 Corinthians 12)*

There has always been an acceptance of the gift of healing in the Catholic Church but this has tended to be restricted to the lives of special saints or to places like Lourdes. Through the charismatic renewal, however, the wider healing ministry of the Church is being restored, as ordinary people are finding that if they lay hands on the sick and pray, healings can and do occur.

We are reminded in the letter of St James, Chapter 5: 13-16, "Is anyone suffering? He should pray. Is anyone in good spirits? He should sing praise. Is anyone among you sick? He should summon the presbyters of the church and they should pray over him and anoint him with oil in the name of the Lord, and the prayer of faith will save the sick person, and the Lord will raise him up. If he has committed any sins, he will be forgiven. Therefore confess your sins to one another and pray for one another, that you may be healed. The fervent prayer of a righteous person is very powerful."

The Sacrament of the Sick

This understanding was incorporated into the sacramental system in the early Church and the Sacrament of the Sick was instituted with the expectation that healing would happen. As time went on, however, the sacrament became less and less used to pray for physical, mental and spiritual health, but was rather seen as the final blessing of the Church before someone died. In the last two decades, however, the true nature of the Sacrament is being rediscovered. The theology behind the gift of healing is that as Christians we are called and equipped to do all the things that Jesus did on earth, and one of the most important of these is to heal the sick.

It was through meeting with Pentecostals who had no sacramental system and where everyone prayed for healing as a matter of course, that lay Catholic Charismatics began to be open to receiving this gift too and started to lay hands on the sick and to pray for healing. People's experience of success in this encouraged them to do it more and certain people discovered they had a particular charism in this area, when the people they prayed for were healed. Of course not everyone who is prayed for is cured, but all those who have the right attitude of trust towards God, experience great benefit from it psychologically and spiritually, even if they are not cured physically.

Regular healing prayer

Some people seem to benefit from what is known as 'soaking'- healing prayer, and become healed after being prayed with regularly for some time. Dom Benedict Heron, a Benedictine monk, who is involved in a healing centre in north London tells how a doctor was healed of

terminal cancer some years ago in this way. For others
the healing is instant. Although I don't have a charism of
healing, I do remember how, once a friend and I prayed
with someone with a cataract condition. To our surprise
the woman was healed and was told by her doctor that
she no longer needed an operation. Another friend of
mine, a nurse, had one leg three inches shorter than
another, due to a pelvic malformation, which caused her
severe back and shoulder pain. She was prayed with by
someone with a healing charism, and watched in amazement as her leg lengthened before her eyes. Since then
she has had no trouble with her back. Charles Whitehead,
one of the leaders of the Catholic Charismatic Renewal in
this country, tells how one of his sons, Luke, was healed
of high frequency deafness as a small boy, when he had a
spirit of deafness cast out of him by a Pentecostal minister who visited the family home. Another dramatic healing which took place in full view of a large crowd happened at the Celebrate conference in 1999, when a
woman crippled by arthritis, was healed and got up from
her wheelchair during a healing service there.

A friend of mine, Benny Blumensaat, as a young man
was an alcoholic and pyromaniac, (an uncontrollable
impulse to set things on fire) and was in and out of mental
hospitals for years, until one day a priest came to visit
him and prayed over him for healing and deliverance.
Benny comments, ""Jesus in one moment did what social

workers, psychiatrists and priests had been unable to do. He healed me and set me free. Not only was I psychologically healed but I was even cured of alcoholism." He eventually went on to train for the priesthood and now is a parish priest in Denmark.

Jan Knight a medical doctor from Taunton said her eyes were opened to God's healing ministry when she was healed of depression through prayer. She comments, "I was also cured of epilepsy through the reception of the Sacrament of the Sick. This started my journey of discovery into the healing ministry. A journey which continues today as I realise we will never fully understand the mysterious ways of our loving God to heal his people." Her experiences and those of others in the Clifton diocese led the Bishop to set up a committee for health and healing in the diocese to help parishes move forward and integrate the healing ministry in its widest sense into the normal life of the parish.

Healing and evangelization

Although there are many minor healings that take place all the time when people are prayed for, as a rule spectacular healings and great miracles are less common in the western world where the secularised and sceptical outlook somehow seems to inhibit the powerful working of the Holy Spirit in this way. The charism of healing can be extremely useful in evangelisation and social transformation too. A wonderful story is told by Fr Emiliano Tardiff, (now deceased) a Canadian missionary who worked in the Dominican Republic for many years. He had a powerful healing ministry which he used to operate, mainly through words of knowledge, when God would communicate to him in an interior way, the healings the Spirit was doing. During one healing service in the town of Nantua he felt someone was being healed of cancer, but no one came forward to claim their healing. Later the person did. She was a prostitute and had been ashamed to admit she was in the church. As a result of her healing not only did she come to conversion but she began evangelising her fellow prostitutes by telling them what God had done for her. At the end of a year, a retreat was held for 60 prostitutes, at the end of which 29 of them gave their lives to Christ and left their way of life. Within three years 80% of the 500 small brothels in the town, which was known as the town of prostitution, had closed down.

Dr John Bonnici Malia, is a Roman Catholic medical doctor and the leader of the Maranatha community in Malta. His whole community is geared towards healing as a tool of evangelisation and his monthly healing services attract between 2000-6000 people on the island. He comments, "Although I gave my life to Jesus when I was 17, I realised that something was lacking. I wanted to evangelise and preach the gospel but I didn't have the power to do it until I was baptised in the spirit. I agree with the

American charismatic leader John Wimber when he says
"to heal is to evangelise". When people are in need and
they see their needs being met by a loving father, they
automatically turn to Jesus."

He adds, "When we started our healing services, faith
in Malta was at a very low ebb. The government was very
against the Church. The healing services we did brought
hundreds of people back to the sacraments. I always
stress that although we should expect physical healings,
the most wonderful healings are the spiritual healings."

He continues "Since we started we have begun to realise
how strong the spiritual battle is in this life. If we give a
foothold to Satan, especially in our own lives or if there is
division in the community or lack of love or forgiveness,
then Satan can work havoc in the healing services. There is
less healing and the words of knowledge aren't so clear.
We have even had members of occult groups praying
against our work, so we must spiritually prepare very seri-
ously before a healing service. This includes spending a
week of fasting and members of the community who are
taking part are encouraged to go to the daily Eucharist. We
also have a vigil with a Mass in it the night before and
spend some time in the place where the healing service will
take place, praising God and praying over every single
seat. These services are always on the last Thursday of the
month and in the summer we do outdoor services which
encourages tourists and other visitors to come too."

Worship and healing

"I believe that worship is a very important factor in opening people up to healing, as it makes them aware of the presence of God from whom all healing comes. At every healing service we have a small prayer of healing for forgiveness too. Everything I feel is part of God's gift to mankind. It starts with medicine but there is a limit to what medicine can do. Normally I give medicine when it should be given but I also pray with my patients at the pharmacy when appropriate. As well as the big monthly healing service a small team of young men also go regularly to the hospitals or people's homes on Sunday afternoons to pray for people individually. Here we have seen remarkable things happening - cancers shrivelling up and other things."

Inner healing

Prayer counselling or prayer for inner healing, is another area that has been discovered through the charismatic renewal. In this people are encouraged to open up their memories to the healing touch of God to help to heal them of the effects of traumatic experiences or rejection. This often has very beneficial effects, although it should always be done with a reputable and mature Christian believer.

Healing is one of the signs of the kingdom of God and of the time when there will be no sin or suffering. It has therefore always to be seen in this context and be kept in balance with the knowledge that while we are on earth sin and suffering will always be part of our lives, but with faith, even this can be redemptive.

Both these points were underlined by the Congregation for the Doctrine of Faith's guidelines on praying for healing which were brought out at the end of the year 2000 and which are a sign of the growing profile of this ministry within the Church.

Faith

The gift of faith is to have a supernatural assurance about something which God gives a believer to encourage them in a particular situation, particularly a work for the kingdom, which enables them to go on in spite of seemingly impossible obstacles. An example of this would be when Jesus performed the miracle of the feeding of the 5,000, which gave him the confidence to tell the people to sit down, as he prayed over the five loaves and two fishes. This can happen in smaller ways today too. For example on one occasion Mother Teresa was preparing to visit the Lebanon which was then in the middle of an acrimonious civil war. This was stopping her from travelling to one of her houses. She insisted, however, that there would be a cease-fire the following day, which would mean she would be able to travel. And to her minders' amazement this is what happened the following day.

Miracles

Miracles are actions that go against the laws of nature. In the scriptures we have lots of examples in the life of Jesus, such as when he walks on the water in Mark 6:45-52 or he feeds the 5,000 in Mark 6:34-42 or raises from the dead Jairus' daugher *(Luke 8:50-56)* or the widow of Nain's son *(Luke 7:11-17)*. Even today such miracles do happen but they are rare, particularly in the West where our rational mindset and lack of faith in God seem to act as a block to the free flowing of the Holy Spirit. There are stories, however, from Uganda, South Africa, Mexico, India and other places of people being raised from the dead or other extraordinary healings taking place. I once interviewed a South African pentecostal pastor called Joseph Kobo, whom God had used to raise three people from the dead. People were always wanting to hear him talk about these spectacular healings but interestingly he himself preferred to stick to more prosaic matters, like faithfulness in prayer, as he saw such miraculous events, simply as signs for the moment, not things to dwell on.

Discernment of Spirits

Discernment of spirits is a very necessary gift when people start to become more aware of the supernatural in their lives, as some striking supernatural healing powers and phenomena can have a human or even evil source. Paul for example recognises that the oracular spirit in the slave girl at Philippi in Acts 16:16-18 is of demonic origin, even though what she shouts out about them is true. Paul likewise in Acts 13:4-12 denounces Bar Jesus, the false Jewish prophet he and Barnabas encounter in Cyprus. Supernatural power in itself is not a sign of God's action but rather love, humility and service. And today too there is always a danger that so called charisms can be used as a source of power and control, which is why the Church has always been cautious of them, and why they always have to be used in the context of community and in an attitude of obedience and submission.

Discernment of spirits is also especially needed in the deliverance ministry whereby a person prays for the healing and release of evil spirits that are causing a person suffering of different kinds, whether it be depression or physical and emotional pain of some sort. In Jesus's own ministry it is evident, in some cases he prayed for deliverance from evil spirits and in others for healing. In Luke 9:37-43, it is stated that the boy has a demon, and in Luke 13:10-13, the cause of the woman being unable to stand up straight is attributed to a spirit, but later on when he heals the man of dropsy *(Luke 14:1-6)*, or cleanses the ten lepers *(Luke 17:11-19)* or heals the blind beggar *(Luke 18:35-43)* there is no mention of these conditions having a demonic cause. Sin also seems to be the cause of some illnesses too, as when Jesus heals the paralytic and tells him to go and sin no more. With apparent mental illness discernment is very important and one needs to know whether the cause might be a chemical imbalance, psychological and emotional problems or whether there could be a spiritual reason behind it. The same can be true even of physical symptoms, which can have emotional or spiritual causes, as well as the more obvious roots. With more and more people innocently becoming involved in occult practices, spiritual oppression is a growing problem that needs prayer and not medication. A simple prayer for deliverance can release people from areas in their lives over which they seem to have no control

CHARISMATIC RENEWAL AND ITS EXPRESSIONS

Prayer Meetings

For a long time one of the ways in which people have encountered Catholic Charismatic Renewal has been through weekly or monthly prayer meetings, either ecumenically or parish based. These tend to be a mixture of fervent singing, sharing of meaningful scripture passages, spontaneous prayer and personal spiritual experiences and insights. Depending on the group there are also times of singing or praying in tongues, prayers for healing and some of the charismatic word gifts like prophecy and words of knowledge or wisdom. (See chapter on Spiritual Gifts at page 26 for a further explanation of these).

One of the primary focuses of the charismatic prayer meeting is praise and worship of God, either through singing or the recitation of psalms of praise. At a time when we have become increasingly rational and task-centred this can be seen as escapism. Prayer of this kind, however, is a call to people to remind them that God is powerful, and holy and worthy of praise, and however bad things are "all things will work to good for those who believe," as God is in control of the lives of his people and the planet.

Charismatic prayer meetings in Britain are known for having a particular kind of music in a pop/folk/rock style. This, however, is not intrinsic but has merely arisen out of the popular music culture of our time, as those touched by the Holy Spirit have sought to find musical expression for their new found faith. In France the music style is quite different. Here it is influenced by the Orthodox tradition and Gregorian chant and much more traditional in form and content. But whatever the outward form, the underlying spirit is the same. It is the music of a people who want to praise God with their whole hearts, their minds and bodies. Hence the bodily gestures - not obligatory - of clapping and raised arms.

Experiences, teaching and kerygma

Because of the conversion that has often been experienced in the lives of many of the people who attend prayer meetings, and the emphasis on sharing these faith experiences of what God has done, there is often a sense of excitement in the gatherings. The Catholic tradition in the past tended to encourage people to keep quiet about their spiritual lives and relationship with God. Those touched by Charismatic Renewal, however, have a deep desire to share with other people their experience of God: both how he has worked in their lives and in the struggles they face with sin and brokenness. The sharing of this in a group helps community to grow among people who normally would not have much in common. The Holy Spirit can use these little testimonies to free people too, as often someone will think they are the only person in the world struggling with a particular situation. Then at a prayer meeting they might hear that someone else has experienced exactly the same thing.

Prayer meetings often have a teaching dimension too, depending on the spiritual maturity of the leaders of the group. This can range from teaching people how to pray for the sick, to explaining Church teaching or to exhorting people to evangelise or to Scripture reflection.

One of the sources of strength and growth in the Charismatic Renewal and in the other lay movements and new communities in the Church is the emphasis on proclaiming the kerygma, that is the core good news at the very heart of Christianity itself. This keeps the dynamism of the community alive, as people are able to share in the joy of new converts while perhaps going through a dry spiritual time themselves.

Praying for healing, physical and emotional, is also part of many prayer groups. This is seen as an extension of people's relationship and trust in God, in that everything is brought to Him. Sometimes there can be quite amazing healings. These are signs of the power of the kingdom of God and the fullness we can expect when there will be no more pain, suffering and sin. Dramatic physical healings, however, are not so common, although they do happen.

Nourishing the charisms

Even within charismatic prayer groups there is a danger that the charismatic gifts start to die out. Charisms die for many reasons. The main one is that they depend totally on the action of the Holy Spirit and not on man's skill and control. Thus they must always be exercised in faith, never quite knowing if the Holy Spirit is prompting a person, or whether it is just a human impulse. This element of risk, of the possibility of exposing oneself as a fool means that deep down many people find it difficult to step out in faith and trust that God will act. Yet as those who do use the charisms will testify, to be used by God in this way is also an awesome and faith building experience.

I believe that many people receive inspirations and words of knowledge from the Holy Spirit which they do not always recognise. By belonging to a charismatic prayer group, and hearing other people's experiences, people learn to see the Holy Spirit working in their own lives and how to respond in their every day life situations.

We are living in a time of special grace, and new structures are needed to form and encourage people in their Christian faith. With the break up of families and natural communities, small Christian communities like prayer groups become more and more important in re-building the fabric of our society and making incarnate the kingdom of God, as well as helping us deepen our relationship with Jesus Christ, the Lord of All.

Praying for the Spirit.

Days of Renewal

Days of Renewal are other occasions where people can Charismatic Renewal. These tend to be area based gatherings rather than parish based ones and generally attract larger numbers than a local prayer group. They happen less frequently and have a more transient make up. Here the focus is on preaching and celebration of faith rather than intimate faith sharing. The charismatic newsletter for England, Goodnews carries information about these days and where they are currently being held round the country.

Healing Masses and Services

Another forum where Charismatic Renewal can be encountered is at healing Masses or services. Usually Days of Renewal also have a time for praying for healing. Once again details of these are available through the Goodnews newsletter. Some individuals have powerful healing ministries. People such as Fr Rufus Pereira from India and Sr Briege McKenna from Ireland travel all over the world preaching the gospel and are used by God in the healing ministry. This often takes the form of words of knowledge which are given to them. But they also will lay hands on people and pray for healing.

Conferences and Retreats

One of the best ways of experiencing Charismatic Renewal is by attending one of the many annual conferences that take

place around the country. Once again these are regularly
advertised in the Goodnews. The largest of these, which
attracts several thousand people, is the 5-day New Dawn
Conference, which takes place in the first week of August at
the shrine of Our Lady in Walsingham, Norfolk. This
blends traditional Catholic devotions such as adoration of
the Blessed Sacrament and rosary processions, with healing
services, charismatic style singing, and teaching sessions on
many aspects of Christian living, devotion and theology.
There is also a fully comprehensive programme for children
and young people. Other conferences tend to take place out
of term at colleges of education. These include the
Birmingham Conference, the Spinkhill Conference and the
Forward in the Spirit Conference and the National Welsh
Conference. There are also camping conferences such as
Campers Renewal. Although most of the conferences tend
to be during the summer months, there is also a very popular one that takes place during Easter week, called
Celebrate. This is a family conference which is run on the
site of a holiday camp and offers a swimming pool, mini-
golf and the delights of the beach, as well as a strong spiritual formation programme for over 1,200 people. The children are divided into different age groups and are taught by
experienced youth teams. As location, dates and contact
names for these conferences tend to change, it is once again
best to get up to date details of these from the charismatic
bi-monthly newsletter Goodnews.

With so many time pressures on people, and a general reluctance to make long-term commitment to more frequent events, the conferences have proved a consistently popular way for those with busy schedules to receive some spiritual input. Whereas numbers attending prayer groups and days of renewal have tended to go down in recent years, the conferences have become increasingly popular.

Life in the Spirit Seminars

The Life in the Spirit Seminars have been one of the major tools that have been used over the past thirty years in preparing and encouraging people to open themselves up to the Holy Spirit, in order that they might experience "the Baptism in the Holy Spirit".

The seminars are a seven week programme, based on talks and small group discussions. The themes covered in the talks are God's Love, Salvation, New Life in the Holy Spirit, Repentance, Baptism in the Spirit and two talks giving advice on steps for spiritual growth. A manual called "Life in the Spirit Seminars" published by Servant Publications gives an outline of the talks, with scripture quotes and helpful pastoral advice in running the course. The key to the success of the course, particularly for Catholics, is the concentration on the simple gospel message and the calling of people to make a personal commitment of their lives to God, something perhaps many

Catholics may not have considered, used as we are to responding in a more liturgical fashion to our faith.

Communities

Another expression of Catholic Charismatic Renewal have been the many covenant lay communities that have sprung up over the years. These differ greatly in the levels of commitment they invite from their members and the way they choose to live out their commitment. Some like the Beatitude Community in France, are fully residential and quasi monastic in their life style. Here instead of only celibates living together as with the traditional orders, whole families share in the monastic calling. Other communities such as the Word of God in the USA and the Emmanuel Community in France are very large but not residential, with single people for example living in flats together and families living in their own homes. Sometimes there would be extended households with several single people living with a family. Members of covenant communities, such as the two above, would often tithe (i.e. freely offer one tenth of) their incomes to support other members of the community working full time in pastoral and teaching functions for the group. Like the lay movements, these covenant communities, would have an initiation process, specific formation and formal membership which would be worked out by their founder or leadership team.

Possibly due to an inclination towards individualism in England, fewer covenant communities have developed in England compared to countries such as France or the United States. Covenant communities, as might be expected, are stronger and more numerous in the third world, in Catholic countries like Brazil or the Philippines, than in the west where a tradition of strong individualism makes community life more difficult.

Emmaus Family of Prayer

The Emmaus Family of Prayer in Southport, England, has been one of the most enduring of the English lay communities. The heart of the community are two couples and their children - the Grimleys and the Camerons - who decided twenty five years ago that they would be able to serve God better and more effectively if they lived together in community. By sharing their resources in this way, they provided both a centre of faith and an example which had an effect on the local area. Their shared lifestyle over the years enabled one of the community to work full time for the promotion of Charismatic Renewal, through a teaching tape ministry as well as providing local leadership, while another ran the home and the other two went out to work and earned an income. Various meetings and activities were run from their house in York Road and a magazine called Agape was produced for ten years. The community has

always had a strong ministry to priests by providing a
Christian family home for support and relaxation. In
recent years this has led to them being asked by the
bishop to help run a parish with one of their priest members in the centre of Southport. In 1997 they also joined
forces with the de Montford Fathers to help with the
running of Sandymount, a retreat centre in
Blundellsands on the Lancashire coast. Apart from the
core community, the Emmaus Family of Prayer is not
residential with no formal covenant commitment and
members show their allegiance merely by attending the
community's monthly Agape Mass or by taking part in
the various community initiatives.

House of the Open Door Community

Another charismatic lay community that has endured has
been the House of the Open Door Community based in
Childswickham in Worcestershire. This is a residential
community of about 35 people, including families and
single people. Originally based in a drug area in Slough
where it had a ministry to alcoholics and those in need,
for the last ten years it has run a farm on the edge of a
small village in the Cotswolds. Here it runs a retreat
house for church groups, discipleship courses for young
Catholics, particularly from Eastern Europe, and regularly sends teams to proclaim the gospel in music and drama
in schools and prisons.

House of Prayer and Formation

Another fruit of the Charismatic Renewal has been the growth of houses of prayer and retreat and formation. Once again these have expressed themselves in different ways according to the individuals involved.

The Brentwood House of Prayer

"Abbotswick", the Brentwood House of Prayer grew out of the vision of one nun - a Franciscan headmistress. After she was baptised in the Spirit she felt a calling to step out in faith into a new area of ministry - that of prayer. She had no resources but with the permission of her order and the local bishop she responded. Her first house of prayer was a small terraced house loaned by another order. When this was outgrown a couple of years later, she managed, through divine providence, to buy a large house with extensive grounds outside Brentwood in Essex, where she was joined by two more sisters and eventually a priest chaplain. Over the years a small network of lay people has formed to help support the work. The house acts as a retreat and prayer centre for the diocese promoting prayer of all kinds and retreats.

Catholic Bible School

The Catholic Bible School is the inspiration of a Catholic couple, Joan and Michael Le Morvan, two further education lecturers. Involved in Charismatic Renewal for many years they initially felt called to set up a community-based centre for healing. This fell through but was part of the process that led them, ten years later, to set up a Catholic Bible School instead. This is a small centre based in an old farmhouse near Chichester which offers short courses on the bible, as well as counselling and spiritual direction. They also run SOS Prayer Line manned by volunteers. The school has strong links with the Holy Land, and every year Joan leads two pilgrimages there, for scriptural fieldwork and meditation on site.

Evangelistic Mission Teams

A desire to share one's faith and the wonderful things God has done is a direct result of being baptised in the Holy Spirit, and has led many touched by Charismatic Renewal to become involved in evangelism, either informally in their local parishes, or by joining one of the growing number of mission teams that have sprung up over the last few years.

Sion Community

The Sion Catholic Community for Evangelism was one of the first evangelisation ministries to emerge from the Catholic Charismatic Renewal. The inspiration of Fr Pat Lynch, Sion was formed in 1986 when he brought a religious sister and three married couples together to form a team to give parish missions. This helped to underline that it was not just priests who were called to evangelise but all

the baptised. Many people of all ages have been attracted
to join the community for shorter or longer periods of time.
Here they receive both formation and the opportunity for
mission without the life long commitment demanded by
religious orders. Today Sion runs school missions as well
as parish missions and trains people in evangelism at their
headquarters in Brentwood. A recent development has
been offering an even more short term mission possibility
by giving volunteers the opportunity after a weekend training course, to join them for a week on mission and take
part in the house to house visitation programme. In this
way they hope to encourage ordinary Catholics to evangelise in their own parishes through faith sharing and witness.
They also run an annual discipleship formation school for
English and foreign students at Brentwood.

The Upper Room Community

One of the hallmarks of Charismatic Renewal is its fluidi-
ty and the fact that it is more concerned about helping
individuals than about the expression of these changes in
new organizations and communities. Some communities
or ministries, for example last for a time, and then dis-
solve freeing those involved to go on to new things. The
Upper Room community would be an example of this.
This was a youth community that existed for ten years or
so from 1987-97 in the St Albans/North London area.
This grew out of a youth prayer group that met in the
mid-1980s following the conversion of a group of friends

feeling the need for a more committed lifestyle and
intense spiritual life than was available in their parishes.
Small groups of single young people began living together in flats, eventually graduating to a larger premise
leased from the Westminster diocese. Employing at one
time three full time workers funded by the tithing of their
members, the community ran large youth outreaches in
the north London area, running various youth events and
small group programmes. These acted as a valuable cata-
lyst for the evangelisation of young people disaffected
from parish life and at its height the community had
about 80 members who covenanted their time and money
on a yearly basis.

As the years went by, however, and the enthusiastic
single young Christians got married - often to each other -
and started having families the intense work load of the
community's youth outreaches and internal maintenance
became too much and in 1997 the community disbanded
to a more loose network of friendships without any formal structure. Some then went on to work full time for
the Church in different capacities while others brought
the skills and commitment they had acquired through
their community experience to normal parish life.

Bible Alive

Bible Alive, is another example of a fruit that has
emerged from a community experience. This very suc-

cessful Catholic devotional magazine (circulation about 26,000 per month), was started by a group of committed Catholics who had all been involved for a time with an American covenant community called The Mother of God. Using the experience they gained with the Mother of God they eventually produced their own publication, which serves not just the Catholic Charismatic Renewal but the whole Church.

WHAT THE CHURCH SAYS ABOUT CHARISMATIC RENEWAL

One of the first high profile supporters of the Catholic Charismatic Renewal was Cardinal Leon Joseph Suenens one of the four moderators of the Vatican II Council.

Interestingly before he ever met a concrete expression of the Charismatic Renewal, Suenens had championed the idea of charismatic renewal. During the Vatican II Council there had been an intense debate between Cardinal Ruffini and Cardinal Suenens on whether the charisms should be mentioned in *Lumen Gentium* (the major document of the Council on the nature of the Church). Cardinal Suenens in his memoirs *'Memories and Hopes'* remembered that Ruffini "asked that the word charisms be suppressed. He felt that charisms were all very well in the primitive Church, but their mention as something that might well still be relevant today could easily lead to abuses. I felt to the contrary, that this mention was necessary, and that the charisms of the Holy Spirit are an integral part of Christian life and evangelisation."

It was Suenens' intervention that the charisms were for all the baptised that carried the day, and ensured a positive mention in *Lumen Gentium*.

Lumen Gentium

"It is not only through the sacraments and the ministrations of the Church that the Holy Spirit makes holy the People of God, leads them and enriches them with his virtues. Allotting his gifts as he wills *(cf. 1 Cor 12.11)*, he also distributes special graces among the faithful of every rank. By these gifts he makes them fit and ready to undertake various tasks and offices for the renewal and building up of the Church (*Lumen Gentium* II.12)."

This was a perfect example of the power of the Spirit working through the hierarchy to support the charismatic dimension of the Church. Thus when the Charismatic Renewal, began to sweep through the Church several years later, the way for its acceptance had already been prepared, and there could be no theological objections to the charisms, for they had already been enshrined in official Catholic teaching.

Thus although individuals - priests, bishops and lay people - then and since have had problems with certain manifestations of the Charismatic Renewal these have been of a more pastoral rather than theological nature. Both Pope Paul VI and Pope John Paul II have supported the Charismatic Renewal. Pope Paul VI called it "a chance for the Church and a chance for the world", when he met catholic charismatic leaders in 1978. There is a publication called '*And Peter Stood up...*' published by ICCRS (International Catholic Charismatic Renewal Services), which has all the speeches and teachings by the popes over the last 30 years about the charismatic renewal.

Christifideles Laici

A very important document for understanding the Catholic Charismatic Renewal is *Christifideles Laici*, Pope John Paul's document on the vocation and mission of the laity, in which he talks about the importance of the charisms and their place in the Church.

"The Holy Spirit, while bestowing diverse ministries in Church communion, enriches it still further with particular gifts or promptings of grace, called charisms. These can take a great variety of forms, both as a manifestation of the absolute freedom of the Spirit who abundantly supplies them, and as a response to the varied needs of the Church in history. The description and the classification given to these gifts in the New Testament are an indication of their rich variety. 'To each is given the manifestation of the Spirit for the common good. To one is given through the Spirit the utterance of wisdom and to another the utterance of knowledge according to the Spirit, to another faith by the same Spirit, to another gifts of healing by the one Spirit, to another the working of miracles to another prophecy, to another the ability to distinguish between spirits, to another various kinds of tongues, to another the interpretation of tongues.' *(I Cor 12:7-10; 1Cor 12:4-6, Rom 12:6-8; Pt 4:10-11)*

"Whether they be exceptional and great or simple and ordinary, the charisms are graces of the Holy Spirit that have, directly or indirectly, a usefulness for the ecclesial community, ordered as they are to the building up of the Church, to the well-being of humanity and to the needs of the world.

"Even in our own times there is no lack of a fruitful manifestation of various charisms among the faithful, women and men. These charisms are given to individual persons, and can even be shared by others in such ways as to continue in time a precious and effective heritage, serving as a source of a particular spiritual affinity among persons. In referring to the apostolate of the lay faithful the Second Vatican Council writes: "For the exercise of the apostolate the Holy Spirit who sanctifies the People of God through the ministry and the sacraments gives the faithful special gifts as well *(cf. 1. Cor 12:7)*, allotting them to each one as he wills *(cf. 1 Cor 12:11)*, so that each might place "at the service of others the grace received" and become "good stewards of God's varied grace *(1 Pt 4:10)*, and build up thereby the whole body in charity" *(cf. Eph 4:16)*.

"By a logic which looks to the divine source of this giving, as the Council recalls, the gifts of the Spirit demand that those who have received them exercise them for the growth of the whole Church.

"The charisms are received in gratitude both on the part of the one who receives them, and also on the part of the entire Church. They are in fact a singularly rich source of grave for the vitality of the apostolate and for the holiness of the whole Body of Christ, provided that they be gifts that come truly from the Spirit and are exercised in full conformity with the authentic promptings of the Spirit and are exercised in full conformity with the authentic promptings of the Spirit. In this sense the discernment of charisms is always necessary. Indeed, the Synod Fathers, have stated: "The action of the Holy Spirit, who breathes where he will, is not always easily recognised and received. We know that God acts in all Christians, and we are aware of the benefits which flow from charisms both for individuals and for the whole Christian community. Nevertheless, at the same time we are also aware of the power of sin and how it can disturb and confuse the life of the faithful and of the community.'

"For this reason no charism dispenses a person from reference and submission to the pastors of the Church. The Council clearly states: "Judgement as to their (charisms) genuineness and proper use belongs to those who preside over the Church, and to whose special competence it belongs, not indeed to extinguish the spirit, but to test all things and hold fast to what is good' *(cf. 1 Thess 5:12 and 19-21)* so that all the charisms might work together, in their diversity and complementarity, for the common good." *(Christifideles Laici)*

John Paul II

Pope John Paul II has throughout his Pontificate encouraged an openness to, and understanding of, the importance of the charisms. At his general audience on 24th June 1992 for example he addressed the question of charisms and their role in the life of the Church and in another gathering the importance of prophecy.

In the Catholic Catechism too although there is no precise list of the charisms, they are mentioned generally in several places and some are specially highlighted. For the first time in fact the gift of tongues and the gift of miracles are mentioned (CCC 2003b). The charism of healing also rates a special mention (CCC 1508).

As well as incorporating charismatic insights and experience into Church teaching, the Pope has also been very supportive of the different expressions of the Charismatic Renewal, by granting official recognition to various individual charismatic communities or leadership networks. In 1990 the Pontifical Council for the Laity granted recognition to the Catholic Fraternity of Charismatic Covenant Communities and Fellowships, as a private association of the faithful, and in 1993 gave pontifical recognition to International Catholic Charismatic Renewal Services (ICCRS), an international co-ordinating body for the promotion of Catholic Charismatic Renewal world wide.

In a meeting with the Council members of ICCRS in 1987 Pope John Paul II commented, "As you celebrate

Charles Whitehead receives the approved statutes of ICCRS from the President of the Pontifical Council for the Laity in 1993.

the twenty fifth anniversary of the beginning of the
Catholic Charismatic Renewal I willingly join you in giving praise to God for the many fruits which it has borne
in the life of the Church. The emergence of the Renewal
following the Second Vatican Council was a particular
gift of the Holy Spirit to the church. It was a sign of a
desire on the part of many Catholics to live more fully
their Baptismal dignity and vocation as adopted sons and
daughters of the Father, to know the redeeming power of
Christ our Saviour in a more intense experience of individual and group prayer, and to follow the teaching of the
Scriptures by reading them in the light of the same Spirit
who inspired their writing. Certainly one of the most
important results of this spiritual re-awakening has been
that increased thirst for holiness which is seen in the lives
of individuals and in the whole Church.

At this moment in the Church's history the
Charismatic Renewal can play a significant role in promoting the much-needed defence of Christian life in soci-
eties where secularism and materialism have weakened
many people's ability to respond to the Spirit and to dis-
cern God's loving call."

Pentecost 1998

More recently the Pope underlined his commitment to the
charismatic dimension of the Church by calling together
representatives from the charismatic renewal and all the lay

movements and ecclesial communities to celebrate
Pentecost with him in St Peter's Square in 1998. He used
this gathering to state that the "charismatic dimension of
the church and its hierarchical dimension were co-essential
as it were to the Church's constitution". He also exhorted
the 350,000 people who had gathered there from all over
the world, "Open yourselves docilely to the gifts of the
Spirit! Accept gratefully and obediently the charisms
which the Spirit never ceases to bestow on us."

This recognition of the importance of the charisms by
the teaching authority of the Church is vital, as it
demonstrates to the whole Catholic Church that the
Holy Spirit is not confined to the sacraments and that
the gifts of the holy spirit or charisms are an important
part of the heritage of the whole body of Christ, including the Catholic Church.

New Movements and Ecclesial Communities meet with the Pope in St Peter's Square, Pentecost 1998.

How To Contact Catholic Charismatic Renewal

There is a loose information structure which people can contact to get in touch with the Catholic Charismatic Renewal. This is headed by the ICCRS (International Catholic Charismatic Renewal Services) office in Rome. This provides information contacts and addresses for the CCR worldwide. At national level, most countries have a National Service Committee and in England there is an information office, which has details of diocesan contacts who are able to put people in touch with local prayer groups.

Catholic Charismatic Renewal Information Office
Postal Address; ICCRS, Palazzo della Cancelleria, 00120 Vatican City, Europe. Piazza della Cancelleria, 1, 00186, Rome, Italy
Tel: 39 (6) 698 875 38 or 698 875 65 Fax: 39 (6) 698 875 30
website: http://www.iccrs.org email: info@iccrs.org

Catholic Charismatic Renewal Office, England
Allen Hall, 28 Beaufort Street, London SW3 5AA
Tel: 0207 352 5298 Fax: 0207 351 4486
Goodnews, bi-monthly CCR newsletter, detailing most events, (£11.00 a year or £1.50 per copy plus 50p P&P) from CCR office, open Mon-Fri 11 a.m. to 4 p.m.
website: www.ccr.org.uk email: ccrgoodnews@netscapeonline.co.uk

Tape Ministries

Agape Tapes, Emmaus Family of Prayer, 11 York Road, Birkdale, Southport, Lancs PR8 2AD
Tel: 01704 568334
website: www.emmaus.uk.com

Welcome Recordings, St Damian's Cottage, 6 Upper Ashton Hall
Lane, Deeside, CH5 3EN
Tel: 01244 538393
website: www.welcomerecordings.com
email: paulsoffe@welcomerecordings.com

Good News Books and Tapes, 60 Wickstead Avenue, Luton LU4 9DP
Tel: 01582 571011 Fax: 01582 571012
website: www.goodnewsbooks.net email: sales@goodnewsbooks.net

Communities

Cor Lumen Christi, Highfield House, Chertsey, KT 8BU
Tel: (01932) 565747 Fax: (01932) 567945
website: www.cor-lumenchristi.org
email: corlumenchristi@bigfoot.com
A small residential semi-monastic community made up of families and
single people an hour from London with a wider associate membership
which is non-residential. Runs various outreaches to youth and others.

House of the Open Door Community, Childswickham House,
Childswickham, Nr Broadway, Worcestershire, WR12 7HH
Tel: (01386) 852084 email: Hod@houseoftheopendoor.org
website: www.houseoftheopendoor.org
A farm-based fully residential community of families and single people
which runs a retreat centre, outreaches to schools and prisons and an
annual discipleship course. Close links with Eastern Europe.

Emmaus Family of Prayer,11 York Road, Birkdale, Southport, Lancs
PR8 2AD Tel: (01704) 568334 website: www.emmaus.uk.com
A network of committed families, single people and groups based in the
Southport area, giving fellowship and solidarity to enable people to con-
tinue their various missions. Weekly prayer group and monthly Agape
Mass, and now collaboration in a retreat centre at Blundellsands.

Prince of Peace Community, Sisters of Our Lady of Charity, Redcliffe, Aughton Park Drive, Ormskirk, Lancs L39 5BX
Tel: (01695) 581449 website: www.newdawn.dircon.co.uk
A small residential community, with associate non-residential members. Main ministry the organising of the annual New Dawn conference and related ministry.

Antioch Community, Trevor Perry, The Windmill, 38a Julian Avenue, London W3 9JE Tel: (020) 8993 9654
A network of committed single people and families in an ecumenical covenant community who live in the west London area. Discipleship, teaching and university outreach.

Maltfriscan Community P.O. Box 1967, Sheffield S6 5YY
website; www.maltfriscans.co.uk
A network of committed families, single people and priests associated with St Mary Magdalene's parish in Maltby. Charismatic/ Franciscan/Carmelite spirituality. Associated groups round the country.

Anawim Family and Prayer Group, Marist House, 10-12 Partickhill, Glasgow, G11 5BI Tel: (0141) 339 8259
Community that have grown out a large prayer group in Glasgow. Non residential. Stress on healing prayer, prayer and praise, adoration of the Blessed Sacrament and ministry to youth.

°Ark of Covenant Community contact Beryl Gill, 5 Calder Close, Coventry CV3 5PN Tel: (01203) 506220.
Embryonic community will run ministry and healing centre in Potters Green, Coventry. Spiritual direction and counselling available, weekly bible study and monthly prayer group.

Chemin Neuf (French foundation -English branch); contact: Beatrice Bourrat, St Gilda's Christian Centre, The Hill, Langport, Somerset, TA10 9QF Tel: (01458) 250496
email: ccngildas@netscapeonline.co.uk

French foundation - Ignatian spirituality and use of the charisms. Catholic with an ecumenical vocation. Charism: the formation of the individual and reconciliation on all levels. Opportunities for 3 month or one year's formation in the French Alps. Annual international youth conference and Cana weeks or married couples and their children.

Covenant Prayer Community contact Martina and Chris Power, Bethel, 30 Tarnside Close, Smallbridge, Rochdale OL16 2QD
Tel: (01706) 640359 email: CandMPower@Netscapeonline.co.uk
Small community, non residential, that grew out of a prayer group. Focus: Running workshops on worship, charismatic gifts, healing etc for parishes and small groups. Organises monthly Flame gatherings.

Source Group, 43 Desborough park Avenue, High Wycombe HP12 3BG
Tel: (01494) 472875
email: sos.con@lineone.net or brin@ntondys.f9.co.uk
Network of committed families and single people in High Wycombe area that has grown out of a prayer group. Non residential.

Spirit of Truth Community, Hilton House, Cranebrook Lane, Hilton, Staffs SW14 OHA Tel: (01543) 480428 email: spot365@yahoo.com
A network of committed single people and families in the Staffordshire area who undertake evangelisation in all its aspects. Non residential. Runs a small annual summer camp for all ages.

Evangelisation Schools and Communities

Sion Community, Sent, Sawyers Hall Lane, Brentwood, Essex, CM15 9BY Tel: (01277) 215011 website: www.sioncommunity.org.uk
email: admin@sioncommunity.org.uk
A mission-based residential community, which runs a retreat and training centre in Brentwood and sends teams into schools and parishes to run missions. Made up of lay people, priests and religious. Discipleship training course and opportunities to join them on mission.

Nottingham Pilgrims, Presentation Convent, Chesterfield Road, Matlock, Derbyshire, DE4 3FT Tel: (01629) 57704
email: info@pilgrimscommunity.com
website: www.pilgrimscommunity.com
Diocesan based youth mission team. Training given and volunteers come for one year's service in outreach to schools and parishes. Also have a house of prayer in Scunthorpe. Permanent core.

Hexham and Newcastle Youth Mission Team
YMT c/o Bishop's House, East Denton Hall, 800 West Road, Newcastle upon Tyne NE5 2BJ Tel: (0191) 228 0003 Fax: (0191) 274 0432
email: blyth@ymt.org website: www.ymt.org
Can also be contacted via Diocesan based youth mission team. Opportunities for training and outreach for young people, Residential for time people belong to team.

Other Ministries

Catholic Bible School, Nutbourne House, Farm Lane, Nutbourne, Chichester, West Sussex, PO18 8SD
Tel: (01243) 371766 Fax: (01243) 371459
email: info@catholic-bible-school.org
website: www.catholic-bible-school.org
Small bible school which runs one day courses, part-time and correspondance courses on scripture, counselling and spiritual direction.

Cockfosters Healing Centre, Priory of Christ the King, Bramley Lane, Cockforsters, London N14 4HE
Mondays and Thursdays after 11 am Mass to 1.30 pm; 2,30 pm on Wednesdays (not during August) Mass of healing the Family Tree 1st Thursday of the month 8 pm. Tel: (020) 8883 4736 or (020) 8883 2665

Catholic Centre For The Healing Of Marriage, Oasis of Peace, Pensamser Road, Porthmadog, Gwynned LL49 9NY
Tel: (01766) 514300
Centre for marriage courses run by small residential community. Team also available to visit parishes.

Healing Masses

For a full list of parishes which run healing Masses send an SAE to the Catholic Charismatic Renewal Office (see above).

London Day of Renewal at Friends Meeting House (opp Euston Station) 10.30 am-5 pm (Monthly meeting - for dates and speakers contact the Catholic Charismatic Renewal Office Tel: (020) 7352 5298).

Westminster Prayer Group - weekly Friday night prayer group that meets in Westminster Cathedral Hall, behind Westminster Cathedral, Victoria, London at 7.30 pm. First Friday of the month is a healing Mass. Tel: (020) 7352 5298.

Other Useful Addresses

The Catholic Alpha Office, PO Box 333, St Albans, Herts, AL2 1EL. Tel: (01727) 822837 website: www.catholicalphaoffice.org
The information office with details on running the Alpha course in a Catholic context. Speakers available to talk at enquiry evenings and days.

Catholic Evangelisation Services, All Saints Pastoral Centre, Shenley Lane, London Colney, AL2 1AF Tel: (01727) 823803
website: www.catholicevangel.org
Evangelisation ministry that produces teaching videos and cassettes on evangelisation and catechetics, with well known figures in the Catholic Church such as Fr Raniero Cantalamessa OFM Cap, Mgr Mark Coleridge, Dr Marcellino D'Ambrosio, Michelle Moran, David Wells and David Alton.

Maranatha Community, 102 Irlam Road, Flixton, Manchester, M41 6JT Tel: (0161) 748 4858 Fax: (0161) 747 7379
website: www.maranathacommunity.org.uk
An ecumenical network with a ministry of unity, healing and renewal. They organise days, retreats and political and social action.

Bible Alive, Graphic House, 124 City Road, Stoke on Trent, ST4 2PH
Tel: (01782) 745600
email: biblealive@internet-uk.com website: www.biblealive.co.uk
A monthly bible magazine with daily reflections on the Mass readings
of the day.

Conferences

Celebrate Conference (Easter week) Family conference at a holiday
park. Separate programmes for children, teenagers, young adults and
adults. Details from : Celebrate, Open House, Bullstrode Way, Gerrards
Cross, Bucks SL9 7QY
website: www.celebrateconference.org.

Forward In the Spirt held at Stonyhurst College, Clitheroe last week
of July. (NO children). Teaching and spirituality conference. Details Fr
Stephen Wright, St Benedict's Monastery, Convent Close, Bamber
Bridge, Preston Tel: (01772) 902204.

Campers Renewal held on different sites each year - currently in
Wales. Full details Mark Baylis, 124 Prices Boulevard, Bebbington,
Wirral CH63 5LP Tel: (0151) 645 7322.

New Dawn held first week in August at the national marian shrine of
Walsingham in Norfolk in a big tent. International speakers, full pro-
gramme for all ages. Accommodation in bed and breakfast and camping
nearbye. Details:Prince of Peace Community, Sisters of Our Lady of
Charity, Redcliffe, Aughton Park Drive, Ormskirk, Lancs L39 5BX
Tel: (01695) 581449 website: www.newdawn.dircom.co.uk

Spinkhill Family Conference held beginning of August at Mount St
Mary's College, Spinkhill, Nr Sheffield. Details: Yvonne Lazenby, 18
Ryecroft, Tickhill, Doncaster, DN11 9VW Tel: (01302) 742368.

Birmingham Conference held mid-August at Newman College, Birmingham for all the family. Details from Eric Shelton 4 Brakenfield Road, Halesowen, West Midlands Tel: (0121) 550 2389.

Wales National Conference held at Trinity College, Carmarthen Mrs Pat Williams 42 Mur Gwyn, Cardiff, CF14 OHA Tel: (01222) 617374

Ampleforth Renewal Community Conference held the last weekend of August at Myddlelton Lodge, Ilkley. Details from Merle Sutcliffe, 18 Brocklesby Drive, Allerton, Bradford Tel: (01274) 483264.

Note: If any of these addresses are out of date by the time you read this book please contact the Catholic Charismatic Renewal Office in London Tel: (020) 7352 5298 for an up to date list.

CTS
MEMBERSHIP

We hope you have enjoyed reading this booklet. If you would like to read more of our booklets or find out more about CTS - why not do one of the following?

1. Join our Readers CLUB.
We will send you a copy of every new booklet we publish, - through the post to your address. You'll get 20% off the price too.

2. Support our work and Mission.
Become a CTS Member. Every penny you give will help spread the faith throughout the world. What's more, you'll be entitled to special offers exclusive to CTS Members.

3. Ask for our Information Pack.
Become part of the CTS Parish Network by selling CTS publications in your own parish.

Call us now on 020 7640 0042 or return this form to us at CTS, 40-46 Harleyford Road, London SE11 5AY
Fax: 020 7640 0046 email: info@cts-online.org.uk

❏ I would like to join the *CTS Readers Club*

❏ Please send me details of how to join CTS as a *Member*

❏ Please send me a *CTS Information Pack*

Name:..

Address: ....

....

Post Code:..

Phone: ....

email address: ....